Seaside GOLF

by John Betjeman

How straight it flew, how long it flew,
    It clear'd the rutty track
And soaring, disappeared from view
    Beyond the bunker's back —
A glorious, sailing, bounding drive
    That made me glad I was alive.

And down the fairway, far along
    It glowed a lonely white;
I played an iron sure and strong
    And clipp'd it out of sight,
And spite of grassy banks between
    I knew I'd find it on the green.

And so I did. It lay content
    Two paces from the pin;
A steady putt and then it went
    Oh, most assuredly in.
The very turf rejoiced to see
    That quite unprecedented three.

Ah! Seaweed smells from sandy caves
    And thyme and mist in whiffs,
In-coming tide, Atlantic waves
    Slapping the sunny cliffs,
Lark song and sea sound in the air
    And splendour, splendour, everywhere.

dedicated to

all the people who know

It's How You Play

THE GAME

HB
HONOR
BOOKS

It's How You Play the Game

ISBN 1-56292-893-7
Copyright © 2001 VisionQuest Communications Group, Inc.

HB Published by Honor Books
P.O. Box 55388
HONOR Tulsa, Oklahoma 74155

Research, information, and transcripts:
  Mary Ann Van Meter and Annette Glavan

All quotes from current players are taken from interviews
conducted for various VisionQuest programs and projects.

Design by Koechel Peterson & Associates, Inc. Mpls, MN

Photography by Tom DiPace Photography
  (unless otherwise noted)
Tom Henry/KP&Associates: cover, 22-23, 24-25, 30,
  32-33, 34, 38, 42-43, 48-49, 50-51, 52-53, 56

THE PLAYERS
CHAMPIONSHIP

HOLE   1

YARDS   392

PAR   4

"Golf is the hardest game in the world. There's no way you can ever get it. Just when you think you do, the game jumps up and puts you into your place."

BEN CRENSHAW

FOREWORD

Over my nearly 40 years in broadcasting, one of the most enjoyable aspects of this profession has been the opportunity to cover the game of golf. I've been blessed to call some of the sport's historic moments and get to know many of the game's great champions. Throughout it all, I've maintained a healthy respect for this amazing game, and the men who succeed at it. I've learned many a lesson for living along the way.

After all, golf is the ultimate dichotomy. So simple a child can play it well, yet so complicated that the best on the PGA tour can never fully master it. Golf is gratifying, yet exasperating. It satisfies momentarily and then leaves us discontented. It is a precise science, yet an incomprehensible puzzle. It tantalizes and teases us into believing we are larger than the game, then leaves us recognizing how completely vulnerable we truly are. It is that very double-edged sword that, for many, makes golf the world's greatest game.

It's in that same way that golf mirrors life so acutely. In golf, there is always room for improvement. Players are constantly learning, trying new things and attempting to perfect their swings. Progress is the goal, no matter what age or skill level. In golf, one bad day is not a complete loss. Each round, no matter how miserably played, provides at least one hole or one shot that sparks hope for the next time out.

Holes one through eighteen offer different distances, landscapes, hazards and challenges. They test our abilities to hit long or short, and keep it straight; to succeed in a variety of disciplines; to overcome obstacles. Golf is about adjusting and reacting to a variety of circumstances, elements and situations. It is a test of one's ability to retain composure, cool and patience—and not defeat yourself. One hole alone does not win a round, but 18. And not just 18 together, but rather one hole, then another, and another.

Similarly, one shot does not win a hole, but rather a string of shots put together. To consistently build upon small successes and finish strong is the plan, but it can not be achieved by looking at the end, or the past. No golfer thinks about the 18th hole when he stands at the first tee. Nor does he rethink the shot he hit in the water at 13, while preparing to putt at 14. While it is assured each round will generously grant a share of thick roughs, sand traps, out-of-bounds lies, and moments you'd just as soon forget, the beauty of this game is that you can always get back on the course. There is always a second chance. Golf provides a new shot, new hole or new day to get things straightened out, and get headed in the right direction.

The men in this book have become examples for these principles. They have stayed on the course in life as well as in golf. As such, their lives demonstrate what true champions should be. They have realized success without sacrificing their priorities, virtue, or personal integrity. They have shown us that life's meaning is not necessarily found in paychecks or trophies; rather *it's how you play the game* that matters most. They also inspire us all to know that through faith, courage, and determination we can all make it through every round of life and finish the course.

PAT SUMMERALL
Fox Sports

"I never thought about being a player. I went into it much more as being a teaching professional. And some of the members there that I had become friends with put up the money and sent me to Tampa and the next year I qualified for the tour."

LARRY NELSON

WARMUPS
Teeing it Up

"Golf is deceptively simple and endlessly complicated; it satisfies the soul and frustrates the intellect. It is at the same time rewarding and maddening—and it is without a doubt the greatest game mankind has ever invented."

ARNOLD PALMER

Golf. The name of the game is short and simple, yet the challenge is so immense and complex. Even the best players in the world admit that attacking this "game" is as unpredictable as straddling a wild bull—sometimes you just hang on for the ride and hope you still have a grip on things at the end.

Some days on the golf course seem like climbing to the tallest summit. The sense of accomplishment reigns . . . but only for a moment. The fantasy lies in believing you have actually conquered the unconquerable. The reality is, that in a short time, the same apex will be far from reachable.

It has been called "the game of games," yet the idea that golf is merely a "game" is absurd. How many games leave us psychologically exhausted when we are finished? How many games compel us to throw our equipment in a lake? How many games arouse such passion and a rabid compulsion to play? Why is it that we have such a fascination with a game that torments us? What is it about this sport that lures us back, time and again, only to be humbled once more?

Could it be the invitation to attempt to master something we surely never will? Is it the competition against ourselves to be better today than we were yesterday? Perhaps it is the realization that we can play a completely imperfect round and still feel as though we succeeded.

"Golf puts a man's character on the anvil and his richest qualities—patience, poise, restraint—to the flame."

BILLY CASPER

Whatever the reason, this game, adored by millions around the globe, has become the ultimate challenge for even the most beginning player.

From its royal beginnings, golf was initially a game for kings and queens, but now it is a sport played by young and old, rich and poor. It has become a part of the fabric of sports history and our cultural and social underpinnings, as well. Who can forget Alan Shepard launching history's longest six-iron shot from the moon's surface on the Apollo 14 mission?

Recently, technology has taken the game to new levels, and a guy named Tiger has drawn millions of new devotees from across the world. Yet, regardless of these changes and the differing styles of players like Bobby Jones, Ben Hogan, Arnold Palmer, Jack Nicklaus, and now Woods, the essence of the game remains constant. Golf is indeed a supreme test of nerves and emotions, of character and poise, of the ability to remember . . . and forget.

Golf is the ultimate dichotomy—a game so simple that even a child can play it well, yet so complicated that the best on the Tour can never master it. It is gratifying, yet exasperating. It is satisfying, yet not fulfilling. It is a precise science, yet an incomprehensible puzzle. It tantalizes us and teases us into believing we are stronger than the game, then leaves us understanding how vulnerable we really are. But, it is that very double-edged sword that, for many, makes golf the world's greatest game.

"The thing about golf is that there can be only one winner. And there's a hundred and fifty-six guys playing in the tournament. Only one winner comes out of that. So the margin for error in the game is a lot finer than any other sport."

LOREN ROBERTS

"You have success. You win a tournament. Everybody wants your autograph or wants you to do outings and so forth. A couple of weeks later, you've missed a cut and you're forgotten. That's why identity in those terms is fleeting. But your identity with the Lord is everlasting."

BOBBY CLAMPETT

"My brother built a green in our backyard. So I started taking my clubs out there and hitting. I remember acting like the tour players. I'd hit balls onto the greens and announce to myself and everything. And then my dad started dropping me off at the public course. And I just developed a real love for the game."

TED SCHULTZ

"We're all very fortunate to be able to do this for a living. I spent one year working as a pro at a golf club, which I think is a real job. Believe me, this is a lot more fun than that. I feel very lucky to be able to play golf."

TOM LEHMAN

"When you play other sports you almost finish at the age of 30. Now, isn't it nice that you can play golf and be playing very well at the age of 70? It's a game that's played everywhere in the world. It's a wonderful game. It's a great challenge. And one of the reasons I keep playing is because it keeps me young."

GARY PLAYER

Lush fairways and greens seem to echo a warm welcome to one and all. Yet lurking on the fringe are ravenous roughs, starving sand traps, and water hazards—all of which are ball-eaters. These are golf's graveyards, where eagles and birdies frequently die. Golf, therefore, is not a game for those looking to enjoy a day in the sun; it is instead, in the words of many, "a good walk spoiled."

Still, the parallels between golf and life are unmistakable. Avoiding hazards, striving for consistency, overcoming failure, handling success, adapting to circumstances, analyzing situations, making wise choices, and staying on the course are important skills to master to be successful in both "games." Like life, golf is the definitive test of humans against themselves. Success is not made in one shot, one hole, or one day. Rather it is found in the ability to consistently string together several shots, holes, and days in which good decisions outnumber mistakes.

For the true professional this is what the game of golf is really all about. It's not about how many trophies are received, how many big paychecks are cashed, or how many headlines are grabbed. Rather, it's about how one plays the game. It is the dedication to every detail as part of a greater whole. It is seeing the big picture and knowing that championships are not built in a day or a shot. It is realizing that rebounding from poor choices, persevering, and overcoming obstacles can lead to greater victories. That is what golf is all about, just as it is in life.

The men quoted in this book have demonstrated they know how to play the game. They stand as examples of character, driven by something greater than the leader board. They are men who display faith, courage, and determination for every round of life. To them, winning is more than sinking a long putt or signing a scorecard; it's about the way the game is played and the lives they can better along the way.

These men inspire us to know that we can all overcome the sand traps of life. They remind us that amidst birdies and bogies, poor shots and long drives, and missed putts and fantastic finishes, there is a greater purpose. Throughout the unpredictable eighteen holes of life we can all learn how to play the game. And finish the course.

"I love playing competitive golf. I love to be in the hunt of a tournament. I love being inside the ropes with a lot of people around, the cameras rolling, something on the line. That is really what fires me up about playing golf. But the golf part isn't a whole lot of fun for me off the tour."

PAUL STANKOWSKI

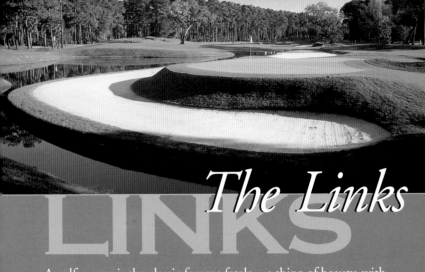

The Links

LINKS

A golf course is the classic femme fatale—a thing of beauty, with hidden dangers. Enticing, yet risky. Golfers attempting to romance her best be wary, lest they wind up in serious trouble. She displays marvelously manicured fairways with tall majestic trees, lush flowery shrubs, and beautiful tailored greens. But silent enemies are lurking—hazards, out-of-bounds markers, bad lies, challenging shots, and trouble spots—all over this vast and varied landscape.

She teases golfers with moments. It's as if she conspires with the ball and clubs to allow the players brief periods of temporary satisfaction. She taunts them by giving them a flickering sense of hope that they may actually conquer the game. It's as if she is providing them with personal moments in the sun . . . just so they will come back again and let her humble them.

"Any hole that has a slight dogleg to the right, that has a bunker short right, like at 260 yards, and then a bunker at 300 on the left; the green has a front right pin. I like those holes."

PAUL STANKOWSKI

"The Japanese have a great saying that "a thing of beauty is a joy forever." I think nongolfers and golfers really enjoy walking around this golf course and feeling the atmosphere of the trees and the flowers and the screaming of the people, the excitement. It's very, very electrifying."

GARY PLAYER

"Golf has afforded me an opportunity permitted few men: to create on one of the broadest canvasses known to man and, in doing so, to complement and, sometimes, to improve on the work of the greatest Creator of all. Golf courses are built by men, but God provides the venues."

ROBERT TRENT JONES

Still, all golfers realize that honor and respect are strictly observed within her bounds, for this is the place where "the noblest of all games" is performed. Herein, participants play by the rules: never walk in the line of another's putt, let the farthest away strike first, and always repair divots and ball marks. They also approach the golf course with dignity, etiquette, and integrity. Some courses like St. Andrews, Augusta, and Pebble Beach can be compared to great places of pilgrimage. They are revered sites where history has been made, and masses gather there, paying homage to the game's past, while hoping to see the coronation of new royalty. Players understand well that the course is to be esteemed, not taken advantage of. They realize that they are today's caretakers of yesterday's heritage and purveyors of tomorrow's legacy.

"Every week we play at golf courses surrounded by trees and nature. All you need to do is look around and know there is a Creator. You know this isn't all pure chance."

SCOTT SIMPSON

THE BAG

It's in the Bag

The tools of trade for this game have changed over the years since European royalty first whacked an orb of feathers with a stick. Yet for all the technological innovations and strategic complexities, one aspect of this game remains unchanged. It is still simply a matter of striking a ball with a club.

Golf clubs are interesting weapons of this trade. What other piece of sporting equipment can cause a player to throw it into a lake in the heat of the moment and then quickly dive in for retrieval? Clearly almost every player navigates a tumultuous love-hate relationship with those fourteen clubs peeking their heads out of the golf bag. How tempting it is to blame our substandard shot making on these sticks of betrayal! Wood, iron, putter—each, when gripped in heroic hands, becomes thirteen ounces of unpredictability.

"When I was a rookie in '82, everybody had wooden drivers, wooden three-woods. Now they're called metal woods. The golf ball is a lot longer these days. They last longer. Irons are better. Everything's better. That's why you see a lot of low scores. But at the same time, if you don't strike the ball right, you're not going to play well."

STEVE JONES

"I grew up playing with golf balls that would spin a ton. You could spin them right off the green. Nowadays the balls don't spin as much and fly a lot farther. The clubs are more forgiving, and the shafts are lighter so you get more club head speed. The changes have equaled a lot of players out and helped me to hit it up there pretty much as far as I need to play competitively."

CRAIG KANADA

"The balls are hitting longer. The clubs seem to hit it farther and straighter. But on the other side they are making courses longer, and the greens are getting harder and faster which makes it harder to score. The hole is still the same size, which is a good thing. But it's still golf. And regardless of how much easier it's getting, it's still a pretty darn hard game."

PAUL STANKOWSKI

And what of the golf ball? Has there ever been an object so small that has caused so great a commotion? This sporting time bomb is just a few blades of grass more than one-and-a-half inches around, and it is lighter than two ounces. Yet, it would be easy to assume that this tiny villain is a foe for the ages. Sure it can travel at 250 feet per second, but where will it go? This little white ball is the game's largest obstacle. Players strive to exercise power over this seemingly insignificant ball, and if they fail to do so, inevitably the ball will exercise power over them.

In the modern era, these accomplices to frustration have become part of a big business and a bevy of choices. Cavity weighting or perimeter weighting? Flexible or firm shafts? Graphite, steel, or bubble? Jumbo heads or titanium? And on and on. All players look for that little extra edge to shave strokes off their games. They want clubs that will give maximum distance and accuracy, and they want balls with increased spin that will fly farther.

Gloves, shoes, training aids, video camera, swing helpers— you name it, and the best in the game have at least given it a try. Yet in the end, it all comes down to two simple things: a ball and a club. In the right hands, it might as well be a violin and bow. At the height of his or her game, one of golf's masters can, for a moment, keep the ball and club under control. The resulting display can be a virtuoso.

"The ball is hotter than it used to be. But I think the driver makes such a huge difference in how far the ball is going and how far especially the ones that are off center go."

TOM LEHMAN

The Swing of
THINGS

Residing within every golfer is a beautiful swing, not just a dysfunctional effort to hit the ball. When executed properly, the swing is a display of true athletic grace. The swing is a powerful action, yet it appears to be effortless. It is controlled finesse rather than uncontrolled power.

Fundamentally, playing golf begins and ends with the swing. It is the foundation of all success. It is an unbroken motion, a rhythm. To break it up into specific parts is to destroy that rhythm. The best swingers know that while there are specific elements to work on, the golf swing is, as Ken Venturi once said, "a composition, not a medley."

"Golf is most assuredly a mystifying game. It would seem that if a person has hit a golf ball correctly a thousand times, he should be able to duplicate the performance at will. But such is certainly not the case."

BOBBY JONES

> *"My swing is unique to me, and it's all a feel thing. The club has to feel right. My swing is a bit of an original, but it works, and it repeats. That's really what you're after—a swing that repeats. So no matter what it looks like, if it repeats, great. If it doesn't repeat, you know you'd better start working harder."*
>
> TOM LEHMAN

> *"I am certain that there can be no freedom, and no natural swing in hitting the golf ball, if the mind is occupied by instructing the body."*
>
> J.H. TAYLOR

The fundamentals of the swing are such that each detail demands proper attention—the stance, the grip, the address. The proper placing of the feet and hands, and the ease of the stance are what the swing is built upon. If the setup is correct, even a mediocre swing can result in a well-placed ball. If the set-up is incorrect, even the greatest swing will produce a lousy shot. The grip is also extremely important. Great players don't just hold a club, they caress it. They feel their hands and the club becoming one.

The swing is made up of four parts: take-away, downward motion, point of impact, and follow through. Each component is memorized by the brain and muscles and practiced so it can be performed automatically and consistently.

The golfer must feel the swing revolve in a circle around his or her spine. The hands must turn in a way to form an inner circle, with the club head forming an outer circle. Both must move in harmony. One ahead of the other means a slice or hook. The body must also flow together. Hips can't open up too soon or too late. The entire body must be working—in all its parts—uniformly.

"If your ball has moved one inch, that can change everything in your swing because then you've moved your arms to move the club head which can change your grip. And that then changes your takeaway. And once you change your takeaway, then you change everything in your swing. And the ball moves differently. Then, if you start aiming incorrectly, you have to make another fault in your swing to get the ball back on line. They just start adding up."

LEE JANZEN

"I didn't start playing golf until I was 17 years old. I got out of college and I really didn't know what I wanted to do. So I became the assistant pro at the country club just for the heck of it. And a gentleman came into my life who really molded my career for about 14 years. I have him to thank for putting me out here because I basically came from nowhere. I was a club pro."

LOREN ROBERTS

"Nowadays you want a swing that's going to hit it far. And then you need to learn to hit it a little straighter. But when you hit it far, you don't have to hit it as straight because you're hitting wedges and nine irons out of the rough, which is a big advantage over hitting a four iron out of the fairway. There's a huge advantage being able to hit it far."

SCOTT SIMPSON

"You start tinkering and all of a sudden you're going to get worse. The game is very simple. There's no reason to over-think. You can think about where you want to hit it, how high you want to hit it, what kind of shot you want to hit. That's fine. Overload comes when you start thinking about your swing. Where you want to be on your back swing. What kind of position do I need to be in? Those are distractions. And the fact is you need to hit a good golf shot."

PAUL STANKOWSKI

Also, the take-away or back swing can't be rushed. Hitting the ball far is a by-product of smoothness of swing, not force. It is like a pendulum, maintaining its tempo, hour after hour. It's about patience. From there, the swing is one unbroken thrust from downswing to follow through. Then, at impact, the club head is whipped through the ball with the hands. The best hitters move their hands faster than others do through the hitting zone. They produce what is called "timed force."

Watching Tiger Woods swing is like watching a bird's flight, a ballerina's pirouette, or a thoroughbred's gallop. It is the coming together of these elements at the height of effortless athletic prowess, and it can be breathtaking.

HOME *on the Range*

Practice, practice, practice is the key to a good swing. Like riding a bike, playing a piano, or performing a dance routine—it is repetition that makes one more skilled in swinging a golf club. Many golfers practice playing imaginary holes in their heads. They also practice taking difficult shots of all lengths, from challenging angles and lies. Oftentimes they do all of this under the attentive eye of an instructor who may choose to introduce training aids or videotape to assist—all in an effort to find the perfect swing.

The game requires dedication and daily attention to the little details. Changes require patience, experimentation, muscle training, and discipline. In golf, as in life, it is more difficult to break bad habits than to learn good habits from the beginning. But simple adjustments in the swing can lead to successfully making difficult shots. So, in slumps, golfers often go back to the basics and re-examine their habits. That is when they head to the practice range or the putting green. Hour upon hour they will work on their swings—driving, chipping, and putting—trying to stay consistent.

"What I've tried to learn over the years practicing is to get my swing simple enough that I only think about one thing."

LEE JANZEN

"You've got the capability day to day to work with an instructor . . . and show you the difference between yesterday's swing and today's swing. Me personally, I could not handle it if my teacher was with me every day. It'd drive me crazy because I'm so feel oriented. It may help me in the long run but in the short run, it would drive me nuts."

PAUL STANKOWSKI

GEORGE ARCHER

Yet, for all of their value in preparing a golfer to step onto the course, the range and putting green are not really where the game itself can be "practiced." While adjustments can be made there, neither place can truly prepare a golfer for the round at hand. Muscle memory and rhythm are practiced there, but it is much like a baseball relief pitcher warming up in the bull pen—where is the game situation?

To really "practice" the game, one must play the game. It is on the course where shot making is tested, for all of the elements are there—the lie, the weather, the competition, and the pressure. On the course it is all about decision-making, experience, and confidence. These things will not be found on the practice tees or putting greens. They will only be found in playing the game.

"I work very hard at it. I'm one of those guys who practices a lot and spends a lot of time on the golf course. And tries to prepare as well as possible."

BERNHARD LANGER

"What other people may find in poetry,

I find in the flight of a good drive."

ARNOLD PALMER

Off the TEE

"Drive for show" is how the tee shot is referred to in this game. And what a show it is!

In the current era, the game has become a power game. For the spectator, it's all about the long ball— who can out-drive whom and who can drive the ball farther than ever before. Tiger Woods, John Daly, and other power hitters in this game draw rapt attention from the galleries, much as Mark McGwire does at the ballpark. And as with McGwire and his batting practice exploits, these men will gather crowds on the practice tees before and after rounds. Fans continue to be awed by their feats.

"Technology is great.

But you know, I think we

need to make sure we

don't want to go too far."

LARRY MIZE

"Everybody likes to see somebody hit the ball 340 yards. I like to watch Daly and Woods and Davis Love and Fred Couples hit it long. Just like in the old days when Palmer and Nicklaus used to hit it real far. Anything that has any type of distance or power, people are in awe of that because not very many people get to hit it that far."

STEVE JONES

"When I was 49 years old playing against the younger fellas, it was unbelievable how much longer they were hitting the ball. There's so many big hitters now on the regular tour that they should be playing longer golf courses because they have so much more power."

GEORGE ARCHER

The drive is golf's version of basketball's slam dunk or football's long bomb. It leaves onlookers breathless. For the every day "duffer," there is no greater thrill than to go out to the tee and crush one like the pros. Perhaps that is because it is the one thing so few can do. While many can chip and putt like the stars of the Tour, few can hit it straight and far off the tee.

With advances in technology—metal woods, titanium shafts, and tighter balls—the game now has a great deal to do with distance from a spectator standpoint. But the one who is longest off the tee is not necessarily the one who is first to the hole. Winning has always been, and always will be, about accuracy. Even today, hitting it straight is still paramount to hitting it long.

"It's more of a power game now than ever. Courses are four and five hundred yards longer now than they were when we came on tour. I know statistics will tell you that the ball goes further now by a dramatic amount."

LEE JANZEN

"There's probably 20 guys nowadays who can hit it a similar distance, which is incredible to me. But it's happening all of the time. So these guys have a huge advantage. When you look at the world rankings nowadays, the top 10 are all long hitters. They all hit the ball a little farther than the rest of us."

BERNHARD LANGER

The shot off the first tee, in particular, seems to set the tone for the entire day, perhaps even the whole tournament. It is where the golfer's intensity becomes most important. The gaze becomes more focused; the stride more purposeful. Here the subject is on a mission—to conquer every bit of the 7,000 plus yards of massive green expanse. What transpires here can be like a sprinter tripping out of the blocks or a football player returning the opening kickoff for a touchdown. It can make or break confidence, leading to the rest of the day being either all uphill or downhill thereafter.

At the first tee it's like a new beginning. The golfer, preparing to strike the ball, is filled with hope and anticipation. The freshly cut, lush green fairway spreads its enticing arms wide and says, "Come to me." A straight hit down the middle will instill confidence and make everything appear beautiful, but a hook or a slice on the first swing will send the golfer scrambling mentally, trying to adjust.

"I'd love to be in the top ten in driving distances just so my name would be in the top ten when they show it in the paper. I'd love to hit as far as Tiger, I mean I'd be silly to say no. It'd be great to hit wedges everywhere. But I hit long enough. I do swing hard at it, pretty much all the time whether it's a wedge or a driver. So, I don't leave much in the bag. I just hit it."

PAUL STANKOWSKI

"Technology has gotten the game to the point where many older courses with hazards in their original spots are obsolete. It has required them to move bunkers, hazards, and some tees."

TOM LEHMAN

"All the golf courses on tour have lengthened it probably 100 yards every year just to keep up with the length that everybody is generating now. But, there's also a point of hitting it too far. The fairways are still as narrow as they've always been. And if you hit it too far, then you start running it through the fairway and getting into more trouble."

CRAIG KANADA

PLAY IT
Where It Lies

The bane of golf, as well as its attraction, is having to play the ball where it lies, as it lies. And oh, does it ever seem to be a ball that lies!

Yet the appeal of this game is definitely in its near insufferable challenges. The rough is just that—work against it in frustration, and you're in for a long day. Lakes could better be termed "ball collectors." And it's been said that bunkers are not necessarily places on the course that randomly grab bad shots, but rather they are places that intentionally punish shots that are not good enough.

Hazards appear as treacherous spots in the midst of this serene landscape. They are sports' land mines in a tropical paradise. Sand traps lurk like great white sharks ready to bite and devour. Lakes are reminiscent of great blue whales hoping to swallow their prey. Water and sand are strategically placed merely to frustrate and ruin the day. Their purpose is the total annihilation of a golfer's score and the abject destruction of his or her confidence.

"The game of golf is a very fickle game. You
can hit a good shot and end up in a divot. You
can hit a nice iron and a gust of wind will bury
it under a lip of the trap. You can get a lot of
bad breaks on a golf course. But I guess in life,
too, you can have some bad breaks."

GEORGE ARCHER

"The chances of you hitting a bad shot—
and what you would call choking—
are pretty high. That's what happens
out there. You choke. And golfers are
going to do it a little more often than
other athletes just because the margin
for error is so slim."

LOREN ROBERTS

Hazards highlight players' weaknesses and abilities as well as provide defining moments for them. Here, golfers can rise to the occasion and through resourcefulness, leave with a decent shot and their dignity intact. That, in itself, can be a confidence builder. It's as if the golfers have challenged the course, and in overcoming all the course has to offer, they play on.

Careful plans must be constructed to deal with hazards. Not just how to avoid them, but also how to manage them. Even with the most cautious preparation, all golfers will find themselves engaging in brief interludes with hazards. So, they must get used to getting out of them and find the best way to do so. In short, they must learn to make the most of them.

Hazards show golfers much about themselves. They also provide character for the sprawling green expanse. They are bittersweet aspects of the game of golf, much as they are in life. What would a course be without hazards, but 7,000 yards of mundane grass? Who can't appreciate the clear blue water set just short of the green and stretching alongside the fairway? Or the sparkling white sand encircling the putting surface? Our senses awaken at the beauty and contrast these hazards provide, making their sheer presence bearable.

"The pressure is tremendous because everything resides on one stroke and you know it. But those are the situations that we practice and train for all our lives. We want to be in those situations in tournaments. We learn more from our difficult times than in the good times it seems."

BERNHARD LANGER

PAR
for the Course

Adversity is the very essence of the game of golf. Often, the ability to recover from a bad shot is more important than being able to hit a good one. Expertise at such will frequently be needed. Disasters happen, but they can be overcome. It is important not to compound a challenging situation by trying to rebound from a poor shot with an incredible one. Attempting the near impossible, often means digging a deeper hole. Golf courses can swallow pride in an instant. Recovery means regaining composure, and sometimes laying up is crucial.

"1991, I was motorcycle riding and wrecked out in the desert. I didn't know if I was ever going to play golf again from that injury. It was 2¹/₂ years before I could even swing a club. A lot of people say, 'Why did this happen to you?' Well, I know why it happened. I was a terrible rider. I didn't know how to stop. I just said, 'Hey, if God wants me to play again, I will. There's a reason for this.'"

STEVE JONES

"After I won the Masters, I started putting too much pressure on myself to perform up to some level. While being a Masters champion is all well and good, my significance comes not from being a Masters champion. I'm only significant because God loved me enough to send Christ to die for me, and no other reason."

LARRY MIZE

"I had seven operations. Back surgery, knee surgery, shoulder surgery, wrist surgery. So life has presented a lot of challenges to me. Disappointments, yes, I've had a lot, but also a lot of thrills. I think if you don't have the bad, you never really appreciate the good."

GEORGE ARCHER

"We lost a baby once at 27 weeks, and it was a very traumatic thing. I just can't imagine people going through traumatic things without that relationship that I have with Jesus Christ. And the peace that God knows what he's doing. That His plan is going to see you through."

RICK FEHR

Every golfer's game falls apart at one time or another—whether for one hole, one day, or an entire round. No one is immune from this dreaded experience, from the most novice duffer to the top ten on the Tour. Mentally, a slump can be devastating. When it happens, some throw their clubs; others merely walk away. Most choose to go back to the essentials. They spend hours on the practice tee and putting greens, pulling their games back together. Self-control is paramount. Players must slow down, compose themselves, refocus, and get back to the basic principles.

The reality of the game perhaps is found in one simple fact: no matter how well or how poorly golfers shoot one day, they must always go back to the first tee the next day and begin all over again. Much like life itself, there is always a second chance.

"I've felt as though I should quit and pursue other careers. Shoot, I've been through the Q School (Qualifying School) nine times. That's enough adversity right there, isn't it?"

CRAIG KANADA

"We all go through adversity at times. But if you want to be a champion not only of sports but in life, you've got to overcome adversity."

GARY PLAYER

"Execution is the key. You need to execute your shot. Sometimes you can't control results out here. You hit a shot and a gust of wind comes up and it blows your ball in the water. Think about execution."

PAUL STANKOWSKI

"A hole in one really is a miracle. Baseball you get the right pitch and you know you're going to knock it out of the park. But in golf, you don't stand up there on the tee and figure, 'Well, I'm going to knock this baby in the hole.'"

LOREN ROBERTS

"It is nothing new or original to say that golf is played one stroke at a time. But it took me many years to realize it."

BOBBY JONES

The Shot MAKERS

Golf is a game of skill, with a certain amount of good fortune.

Those who are successful have command of their concentration and focus. They have an ability to survey and analyze, so they know when to play percentages and when to gamble. They exercise good judgment and self-discipline, and their nerves and emotions remain controlled while under pressure. They manage to maintain the sense of timing and rhythm, and they seem nearly always to hit the opportune shot at the necessary moment.

Great players visualize their shots first and trust that they will be rewarded for their countless hours of practice. They have linked the emotional with the physical and have become shot makers. They see the target, feel the proper execution, and trust themselves to achieve.

The legendary Bobby Jones once said, "The real way to enjoy playing golf is to take pleasure, not in the score, but in the execution of the strokes." Shot-makers enjoy playing the game of golf.

"If you don't have that focus on wanting to play each shot one shot at a time, and you're thinking about your victory speech on Friday or Saturday, it's just not going to work out. The best players have always been able to focus on one shot at a time. Whether it's a putt they have to make or their tee shot or whatever, it's really important to think about just that one shot."

STEVE JONES

"Golf is a game of adjustments. I may wake up one day and it's real easy for me to hit fades. And the next day, it's just real easy for me to hit hooks. Everyday is an adjustment. And if you're not able to make those adjustments, then life's not going to be as easy."

LARRY NELSON

Golf, at its fundamental basis, is made up of two types of shots—those in the air and those on the greens. Three things affect the ball's flight toward the fairway: the impact and point of contact with the club, the wind on the ball in flight, and the terrain the ball lands on and reacts to with a bounce or roll. Shot-makers understand this, so they survey the shot, make a plan, commit to that plan firmly, and then execute it. They cannot second-guess themselves. They cannot over-analyze the situation. They must shut off the thinker and release the trained athlete within.

For the shot-makers, each shot is an event in itself. They are aware of their limitations, so they know when they can reach the green in two and when they need to lay up. They adjust as needed—all without taking away any of their aggressiveness.

Instead of thinking about not hitting the shot into the bunker, shot-makers think about driving it down the fairway. Instead of thinking about not slicing the ball, shot-makers think of hitting the pin. Shot-makers are constantly thinking about what must be done to make a successful shot instead of entertaining the fear of missing it.

"You just can't allow yourself to live in the past. You can't let a bogie or double bogie or missed putt ruin your whole day. And that's happened to some of the guys. It happened to me at the beginning of my career. And it still happens every once in a while. We need to learn to forget those bad shots. The next shot is always the most important one."

BERNHARD LANGER

"Sometimes it's good to be a little dumb out there.
Just kind of play and enjoy it because you can think
too much and then it really gets you in trouble."

LARRY MIZE

Galleries

GALLERIES

> "The odds of hitting a duffed shot increase by the square of the number of people watching."
>
> HENRY BEARD

Galleries? Far from galleries these throngs are. Not silent like works of art that hang on museum walls, these fans gasp and cheer, holler and hoot, clap and whistle. Still, are they ever a piëce de rèsistance for the backdrop upon which this game is played!

Most players have a sense of camaraderie with this multitude. They carry on conversations, exchange a glance and a smile, or merely wave. But the best know how to work the crowds, and like comedians, they use the gallery to their advantage. Finding encouragement, a temporary respite from the pressure, or a way to release anxiety, players use the crowd as a positive force.

> "The people get so close to you and I enjoy it. I mean you got to have a little ham in you to play out here. I'd much rather play in front of a couple a thousand people than five or ten. I love to have the fairways lined. I love to play in front of people. It gets your adrenaline going."
>
> LARRY MIZE

> "The gallery can definitely help you along. You really know it when the crowd gets into it, and they're cheering for you and supporting you. I like to make sure that I'm paying attention to the crowd and respond to the crowd. But I'm not a real chatterbox to the crowd, I think you need to use the crowd as your friend."
>
> TOM LEHMAN

The faithful here are made for this game. They love to watch monster drives and extra long putts that clank into the bottom of the cup. They walk the course, following their favorite players over some 7,000 yards of varied terra firma. These fans are truly a part of the golf landscape.

They also relate to their heroes more so than any other fan. While many armchair quarterbacks can second-guess a play, how many fans can recount what they did last week in the same situation? A gallery member watches a putt drop from twenty feet and remembers when he or she did the same, just a few days ago. The association of the fans with their icons in shared experience, combined with their ability to empathize, is what makes this relationship so unique. Perhaps that is why galleries are such a vital part of the environment of this sport.

MOMENTS
in the Sun

The game of golf has quite a revered history. From the early days when the sport was played by kings across the world, to the current reign of the Tiger, there have been many magnificent moments to behold. This generation's stars have held aloft trophies, bearing names of past legends, that have been passed down for decades or even centuries. This reminds us that for as much as the game has changed, its continuity remains. The ongoing link of golf's own storied history is immutably profound.

While names change, every historic course has seen the same shots made today in bygone days of yesteryear. Those shots may have come by the striking of a true wood instead of a bubble shaft, but they have been made all the same, and from the very same spots.

Footprints in the sand trap were first tracked there years ago by a distant predecessor. The shot from the rough, the long putt, and the chip in from the apron—the course has seen them all before. Birdies, eagles, pars, and bogies have all been played out a lifetime or two ago. The special rounds and magic moments have all transpired before. And soon, as if through a transmutation of time, they will occur again.

"The U. S. Open to me was the sweetest victory ever. To happen on Father's Day. To have my wife and two kids run out on the green and hug them. That's what it was all about. Just having the family there and that whole atmosphere, it couldn't have come to a better ending."

STEVE JONES, *U.S. Open Champion, 1996*

BAY HILL INVITATIONAL

LEADERS	HOLE PAR	1 4	2 3	3 4	4 5	5 4	6 5	7 3	8 4	9 4	10 4	11 4	12 5	13 3	14 4	15 3	16 4	17 5	18 4	1ST. RD.	2ND. RD.	3RD. RD.
PERRY C		7	6	6	6	7	7	6	6	6	6	7	7	8	9					71	66	
GARCIA		8	7	7	8	7	8	8	9	9	9	9	9	9	9	10				71	66	
MC CARRON		7	7	7	7	7	7	7	7	8	8	9	9	9	10	11				67	70	
WAITE		7	7	8	9	10	8	9	7	7	7	7	7	8	7	7	8			66	71	
FRAZAR		5	4	4	5	6	8	9	10	10	10	10	10	10	9	8	8			70	70	
JANZEN		4	4	4	4	5	5	6	6	6	7	10	9	9	9	9	9	8		67	72	69
WOODS		6	6	7	7	8	8	9	10	11	11	11	12	12	12	12	11	12		71	67	
MICKELSON		4	4	4	6	6	7	7	7					7	6	7	8	8		66	72	
SINGH		3	3	2	3	3	4	4	4	4	4	4		6	7	8				71		

"I was born and raised in Augusta, and as a youngster I used to work on the scoreboards. To beat Greg (Norman) and Seve (Ballesteros) was just icing on the cake. As well as getting the jacket from Jack (Nicklaus) who was my childhood idol. I just remember going crazy. I mean I started jumping up and down and running all around screaming. It was the ultimate golfing thrill for me."

LARRY MIZE, *Masters Champion, 1987*

"Winning the Masters was a great thrill. I won it in a very close head-to-head battle. Five fellows could have won that tournament in the last three holes. And I was the fortunate enough one to be there and just keep making pars. And that was good enough to win."

GEORGE ARCHER
Masters Champion, 1969

But then golf always has been framed as a game of great moments—Payne Stewart's putt at the 1999 U.S. Open, Larry Mize's chip at the 1987 Masters, Tom Watson's bunker shot, Jerry Pate's dive in the lake, Hale Irwin's high five run, and on and on. The moments leave us with lasting impressions of champions and the days that defined them and completed their careers.

These are days when everything comes together for golfers. They are in the "zone." Each element of their game is functioning and responding properly. Every tee shot travels a little farther and a little straighter. Every approach is on the green. Every putt seems to find the bottom of the cup. The wind is with them. They read every green correctly. Even when they take risks, they are rewarded. These are golfers' moments in the sun.

"I've had two career highlights—one being the British Open victory in '96. But I think maybe the most incredible experience I've ever had on a golf course probably was the Ryder Cup in '99, and being a part of that team victory. There's something special about being a part of a team."

TOM LEHMAN
British Open Champion, 1996

"Winning a Major is something everybody wants out here. To win at Augusta was even more special. And to have won on Easter Sunday— which is maybe the most special day in a Christian's life—and to be able to give Him the glory was very, very meaningful to me."

BERNHARD LANGER
Masters Champion, 1985, 1993

"After you win a few tournaments, everybody acknowledges you as not that great until you win a major. And then I won the PGA. Then I won the U.S. Open. Then I won a third major and there was a lot of satisfaction because this was something that wasn't supposed to happen."

LARRY NELSON
U.S. Open Champion, 1983, PGA Champion 1981, 1987

"I put a scripture in my pocket that week. It was Colossians 3:17, 'Whatever you do, in word or deed, do it all in the name of the Lord Jesus giving thanks through him to God, the Father.' I played all that week just kind of thankful. It seemed to take a lot of the pressure off for me. So that last nine holes, I just tried to play my own game. I finished great and beat Tom Watson. There's not much more that you could ask for really."

SCOTT SIMPSON
U.S. Open Champion, 1987

Short GAME

If the game off the tee is about distance and accuracy, and if putting is about the highest degree of accuracy and delicate touch, then the short game is about regulated strength and accuracy of direction, from all kinds of distances and from all types of lies.

Short shots are most telling of all, for no one can become an effective golfer without a good short game. There have been scores of those who could drive and putt, but their careers died somewhere in between.

Golfers know the 60-60 principle very well. Of all shots in a given round, 60 percent are taken from within 60 yards of the hole. Yet most players are seen only on the driving range or putting green after their round is over. Few have the needed discipline to practice the short game. After all, it is not what impresses crowds, wins wagers, or begets braggers.

"For reasons too obvious to state, of all the shots in golf, the short shots are most telling. No one can become a good scratch golfer without an effective short game."

E. M. PRAIN

"The short game is the key to success. Chipping and putting and getting the ball in the hole quickly is what it's all about. Increasingly we're having more wedges or sand wedges or nine irons in our hands. The guys with the best short games are really rising to the top."

TOM LEHMAN

"You lose some of your skills and power as you age. But you don't have to lose your skills around the short game. You can be a better sand player or a better chipper. There's some fellows I know that are going up in their 80's that have wonderful short games."

GEORGE ARCHER

"The player who recognizes that he needs to devote his head and hands to improving his short game sees the right route to lower scores."

TOMMY ARMOUR

But some understand, and so they do practice it. They realize repetition in the short game is how they train hands and fingers to function effectively. The golfer's head and hands are of utmost importance in the short game, and they can lead to lower scores. As such, short shots are best thought of as miniature drives, with all of the same principles applying—grip the club lightly, stand naturally, avoid tension, feel the club head in your hands, and swing it crisply through the ball.

But the short game also is more than just hitting the ball. Consider an approach shot from forty to eighty yards. Typically, the wind is blowing, and there are hazards on both sides of the green. The pin is placed at the front of the green with a slope up behind. Where does the shot-maker place the ball? How does he or she get it there? What will the ball do once it lands? Where will this shot-maker be putting from?

In the short game, skill, control, and finesse are required, so the best players survey the shot. They consider how to play the hole and what club to use. Next, they determine how hard to hit the ball, where to place it, and what the wind will do to the ball in flight. Finally, they decide whether it is best to draw the ball, fade it, run it up, or try and stick it at the pin.

The ability to answer these questions definitively, make adjustments, and play the short game well is what separates champions from the rest of the pack.

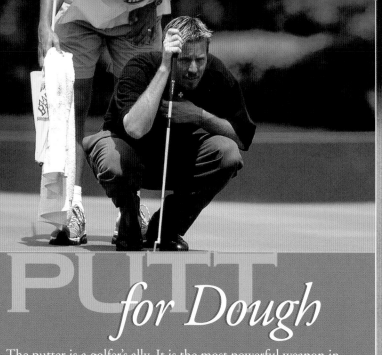

PUTT *for Dough*

The putter is a golfer's ally. It is the most powerful weapon in the golf bag. All golfers know that, while the long drive is what most fans come to see, it is an economical putting game that fattens the wallet. More strokes are made up on the greens than anywhere else in the game. It is on the green where champions are made. The essence of putting is reading the undulating greens, setting the proper stance, staying confident, and mastering what the pros refer to as "the touch."

Putting looks easy. The surface is well manicured. There are no trees or rough. There are no bunkers or water or out-of-bounds areas. The stroke is relatively short and elementary. With all of these seemingly harmless factors, why does putting create so much frustration and consternation?

"Why am I using a new putter?
Because the old one didn't float too well."

CRAIG STADLER

"You don't need strength. You don't need flexibility. You just need a lot of feel. You need good eyes to see the putting line and to read the greens correctly. And then you've got to have the feel for the distance. You need the technique to hit the ball in the middle of the club face and get a good roll. You've got to see it, feel it, and then do it. A lot of that is happening between the two ears."

BERNHARD LANGER

"Obviously the game is much more than driving because if it wasn't, then all you'd need was a driver. But you don't. You have 14 clubs and you use your putter 45 percent of the time. So, obviously the putter is pretty much the most important thing in your bag."

STEVE JONES

"It is confidence and technique. There are mechanics, but I think putting is more mental than the mechanics."

LARRY MIZE

Watch a player preparing to putt. He or she will step back and read the line, address the ball, stop and read the line again, and talk it over with the caddie. Then, the golfer will measure the line with the putter, walk around and observe the break in the green from a number of different angles, and stand over the ball and study it as if it were the Hope Diamond. Seconds turn to minutes, as the player seems to be delaying the inevitable fate. Finally, the golfer summons the courage to strike the ball. When it goes in, his or her demeanor turns to unbridled joy. When it does not, rest assured the disobedient ball has a scolding coming.

Putting a 1.62-inch ball into a $4\frac{1}{4}$-inch hole is far from simple; in fact it can be the stuff of nightmares. To succeed, one must constantly practice. Yet putting is both a fine art and a science. On the greens, the elements that affect the ball's travel are completely different than anywhere else on the course. First, the golfer must consider the degree of the break and the type of grass—tall or short, thick or thin, wet or dry, slow or fast. Then the player must determine the right speed to hit the ball and whether there are any imperfections in the green. All data are calculated as the shot is approached.

"Some days the hole seems about one inch big and nothing goes in.

You have to understand that it's a cruel game. But it's a great game."

GEORGE ARCHER

Putting is about lines—straight, curved, uphill, downhill, slow, fast—and how to use those lines to work for you rather than against you. Reading those lines properly can be the difference between a birdie and a bogie. The putt must be viewed in its whole journey from start to finish, or the shot can't be shaped as a whole. Rhythm is the essence.

Putting is a combination of geometry, botany, physiology, and psychology. A player can drive long down the middle, pitch to the hole, and then putt into a 9-5 job. This is the science of putting, but it is also an art that involves touch, feel, and confidence. Golfers must visualize what needs to be accomplished and execute it to precision. They must read, aim, commit, and then generate a fluid, solid contact from clubface to the hands. When they put every aspect together smoothly and harmoniously, they make the putt. Sounds easy, doesn't it? If only it were.

Without question, putting is more a mental exercise than physical. No one is a good putter without confidence . . . and a short memory. A good putt can be quickly forgotten, but a bad putt lingers. Confidence is the single most important tool the golfer has on the greens.

"You really want to take advantage of it when

your putter is hot and the ball is going in

the hole, because it doesn't last."

CRAIG KANADA

"Confidence has a lot to do with it. I struggle with that. Well, is it because I haven't seen a lot of balls go in the hole? I haven't practiced? Or have I just lost my confidence? I don't know. Ultimately what makes a great putter is that the ball goes in the hole."

PAUL STANKOWSKI

"You've got to have good mechanics to be able to repeat the stroke again and again. But then on the other side, you have to have the confidence to be able to walk out there and trust your mechanics and put the ball in the cup."

AARON BADDELEY

TERMS

ADDRESS Position of a player who has taken a stance over the ball and grounded the club—preparatory to striking the ball.

APRON Area bordering the green, with grass longer than the green but shorter than the fairway.

BACKSPIN Backward rotation of a ball caused by striking it with a downward blow.

CADDIE Someone who carries a player's golf bag, locates the driven ball, and, on occasion, offers advice.

CARRY Distance a ball travels in the air.

DRAW SHOT Shot that travels straight, slightly to the right of the target, then curves inward to the left; a controlled hook.

FADE Left to right direction of a shot, opposite to the draw shot; a modified slice.

FORE Warning cry directed to persons within range of a shot.

HOLE-IN-ONE Striking the ball from the tee into the hole in one stroke.

MULLIGAN Free shot sometimes allowed after a poor drive.

SHANK Shot in which the ball is hit by the heel of the clubface and flies off line to the right.

WINTER RULES Practice of improving the lie of a ball by moving it to a better position because of poor turf condition. Not endorsed by the USGA.

"Nothing puts pressure on you but yourself."

LARRY NELSON

The Game
WITHIN

Above all, the most difficult aspect of the game of golf is the game that is played out within the mind, heart, and soul of the golfer. To play golf means to accept imperfection. One must realize the perfect game never has been played, never will be played, or never could be played. The great Gene Littler once said of his profession, "Golf is not a game of great shots. It's a game of the most accurate misses. The people who win make the smallest mistakes."

Golf is a game made up of errors. One of the keys to succeeding is being able to cope with failure and deficiency. The ability to do so means you can be freed emotionally to play your best. The inability to do so, however, means the fear of failure will reign. Thus, mastering the art of playing golf well depends on mastering the art of playing poorly.

"Golf is a test of temper,
a trial of honor, a
revealer of character."
DAVID FORGAN

"The whole goal of handling pressure is really to
be able to play on Sunday under the gun the same
way you would on Tuesday with friends."
SCOTT SIMPSON

"At times I will be honest with you, I question my ability. 'Do I have enough stuff to play out here? Do I have enough heart or do I have enough game to really do it?' And I think my faith has really helped me deal with that, just going ahead and sticking in there."

LOREN ROBERTS

Many players have what it takes from the neck down to become proficient ball strikers. But it is between the ears, rather than between the greens, where even the most gifted players are defeated. This is indeed the cruelest of mental games; its anguish rips the very soul of those who test it. To be set apart, the golfer must have a mental edge, for while progress is the ultimate goal, the measurement of such can be a rather nebulous prospect. In fact, the draw of this game is this mental challenge. Golf is a thinking-person's sport, rewarding patient players who know they must conquer all eighteen holes to be successful.

"When you're really on top of your game, the pressure never seems to be as much even if you're contending for a tournament. It's when you're not so sure of your game and you've got to get up there in contention, that's when the pressure mounts. You miss a couple of putts in a row and suddenly you're on the cut line again. And you don't want to miss the cut again."

LEE JANZEN

Golfers must have a plan for the entire course—knowing how to attack and what shots to hit—prior to their round. Effective course management means surveying the course and analyzing all options. Success will follow a series of right choices—what club to hit, what chance to take, where to hit it, and what type of shot to play. During play, this superfluity of information must be processed, and decisions must be made within seconds, all without losing focus.

To excel, players must have a keen ability to concentrate and to eliminate all thoughts that conflict with their focus. They must have a true singleness of purpose. If they are emotionally distressed, their tempo will be affected. They will swing too hard, grip too tight, or rush the downswing. To control their games, golfers must first control themselves.

Those who are champions say they have trained themselves to believe that when they stand over the ball, that shot is the single most important matter in their lives for that moment in time. Given the equality of talents on the Tour, the one who can keep everything under control emotionally in a given tournament will be the winner.

"We have a thing called The Yardage Book. And The

Yardage Book for me means two things. One, it's information.

Two, it's kind of a routine. It gets me in my routine. So when the

hole is over and I write the score down. I put that score card

underneath the page. I flip it and now I'm on the next hole.

And I look. How far is it to the next bunker? So now I'm focused

on the next hole instead of what's behind me."

PAUL STANKOWSKI

"Having nerves and feeling pressure just gets you focused and gets your concentration level up to where it needs to be. It's kind of harnessing that nervous energy into a positive way by letting your focus get really narrow and really intense and be in that zone. When it really gets away from you is when you're nervous and your mind starts to race. And you're kind of thinking three steps ahead of yourself. Then pretty soon you're playing lousy golf."

TOM LEHMAN

"My expectations are higher than what anyone else can put on me. And when I don't quite play to that level, it's a bit frustrating. I try and just go there and play one hole at a time. And hopefully end with the lowest score."

AARON BADDELEY

Making the TURN

On the course, each round is comprised of two parts—the first nine holes, known as the front nine; and the last nine holes, or the back nine. Often, playing the front nine seems like scaling a great mountain, while the back nine feels like the descent. In between, golfers experience a cathartic time of transition called "making the turn."

Making the turn has profound meaning for golfers because on the course, no matter what the front nine have been like, there is always hope when hitting the back nine. That is when they make the turn. On a disastrous day, making the turn means heading for better things. On a successful day, it means finishing strong. Either way, the players are heading for home. Golfers know there is security in making the turn. It is a chance to refocus, get a fresh perspective, leave the old behind, and start anew.

"I recognized that I did need to make a turn. I was living a life of sin. And God offered a solution to that in Jesus. That happened to me in college. Obviously the single most important decision that I've ever made."
RICK FEHR

"Sometimes you can be going along in life and not even realize that you're heading the wrong direction until someone points it out to you. My wife just pointed me in the right direction."
LEE JANZEN

"I made the turn in 1984. I started with the whole idea of proving it wrong. And over three years of asking every question I could think of and reading a whole bunch of books, I became convinced that it was true. That Jesus was who he claimed to be. That he was God. It wasn't an emotional decision at all. The only reason I decided to become a Christian was because it was true. I couldn't argue with it anymore."

SCOTT SIMPSON

"The front nine goes out. You're heading out and there's no real destination. Well, once you make the turn, now you're headed back in. You know you're headed home. Well, for me, the front nine was prior to 1986. I was headed out. I really wasn't sure of where I was going. But once I made the turn and accepted Jesus Christ as my Lord and Savior, then I knew where I was headed. I know where I'm going and I have a great final destination."

LARRY MIZE

"The fact is we all fall short of the glory of God. And Jesus Christ is our bridge between God's perfection and our sins. Jesus paid that price for us. It's a free gift. We're all going to spend eternity somewhere. Some of us are going to be in heaven. And some of us aren't. We're not living in the land of the living. We're in the land of the dying going to the land of the living."

PAUL STANKOWSKI

"If your whole life is wrapped up in golf and how well you play is how good you are overall, then you can never ever reach that level of perfection in the game that you would require to make you feel good about yourself."

LOREN ROBERTS

So it is in life. The front nine can represent days, weeks, months, or years. They may have been the landscape for encountering the sand traps of life—failures and tragedies. Yet there comes an appropriate time to take one's focus off of what has been left behind and place it firmly on what lies ahead. This is "making the turn."

In making the turn, one looks toward the security of home. Making the turn is about change. Many pros have experienced the height of success as well as the depth of trial, and they have found that for them making the turn means turning their golf games and destinies over to the One who designed the course for their lives.

"Playing for a living is awesome. But to have a relationship with God, to have a good family and friends and that sort of thing— what else can you ask for? Playing golf is just the bonus."

AARON BADDELEY

"I was taught you had to be good; do lots of good deeds. Hopefully you were good enough that God would let you into heaven. There was always this guilt - was I good enough? Would I make it? I was never sure. It was very clear for me that I had to give my life over to the Lord and trust what Jesus did for me and not what I was going to do for Him. When I made the turn, it just freed me up. I didn't have that guilt anymore."

BERNHARD LANGER

"Am I perfect? No. Do I still make mistakes? Yes, I do. But to make the right turn heading home - following Christ— that's what you want to do. You don't always head the right direction. But He gives you the Bible to help you out and make the right turn towards home. So you'll end up in the right place. That's what God has given me is that security that I know what's going to happen when I die. I have the answer to the six-foot hole."

STEVE JONES

"That's the reason why we were created was to have a relationship with God. That is the only way we are going to be truly happy. Nothing else will fill that void in your life other than that relationship with Jesus Christ."

LARRY NELSON

For these golfers, it is not the Masters, or any other hallowed tournament, that will turn things around. Rather it is the Master himself. They know that just as a club in the right hands means success on the course, their lives in the right hands means victory in life that goes beyond the scorecard.

For them, it is about making the turn to a better way, to a back nine filled with hope and opportunity. It is about following a cart path leading to peace and fulfillment. It is about playing a round in which bogies can be handled more readily, as they see the bigger picture as a part of finishing the course.

One day we all will sign an eternal scorecard at the end of our final round. What will it say? These golfers know their scores will not be determined by how many rounds they won. Rather they will be based on whom they trusted to guide them to finish the course, and how they played the game.

"Joy is not the same thing as happiness, you know. So, if I go out and bogie a down wind par five, I'm not very happy. But it still doesn't steal the joy that I have knowing that I'm in a secure place now and eternally. He's given to me the sense of having the slate washed clean."

TOM LEHMAN

Nineteenth HOLE

"What's my legacy going to be? What are they going to say when I'm gone? What are my kids going to think of me? I want to be remembered as a person who loved people, and that my love for people came from a love for God. It's not so important that people remember me for golf. I'm happy with what I've achieved, but it's more important that my life has meant something and that I've affected other people's lives in a positive way."

TOM LEHMAN

"The fact that Jesus paid our debt for us. Can a human being make that same sacrifice today for the rest of the world? I think it'd be hard for us to find anybody to do that. You can find a family member who would donate organs or die for a child. But would they do that for people who weren't born yet? It's a sacrifice that was made for me. I feel indebted. That love is so big that it's incomparable."

LEE JANZEN

"I've got a joy that's there all the time, that I can only get through Jesus Christ. The game sometimes makes me happy. But the game doesn't bring me joy. Jesus Christ brings me joy. Masters victories are going to come and go and they're going to end. But my personal relationship with him is what will always last and will never die."

LARRY MIZE

"When I keep my eyes focused on Him, it's amazing the peace that I have in my life. Little things don't get to me. That's a great feeling. I never had that before. When you take your eyes off Jesus, you see everything else around you. That's not good because when you see things around you, you forget what you're living for and forget what your purpose is. So that's my objective, to keep my eyes on Him."

PAUL STANKOWSKI

"I know that God loves me. He created me and He knows my weaknesses and my strengths. And He loves me no matter what. Whether I shoot 62 or 82, it doesn't change my value to Him."

BERNHARD LANGER

"With faith in Christ, even in the midst of whatever can happen, you always have hope. You have a hope for better things. I can't imagine living life now without that hope."

SCOTT SIMPSON

WILLIAM *Payne* STEWART

. . . it seems, was born to play golf. He had two elements essential to becoming a star—a vibrant personality and a classic swing. The personality was authentic and incomparable. He was colorful and engaging, funny, personable, and compassionate. The swing, well it was flat out beautiful. A buttery smooth back swing and fluid follow-through made Payne's swing the most graceful and admired on Tour. It was common to see fellow pros standing behind him at the practice tee, speechless, as if they were hoping some of his golfing elegance would rub off on them.

The combination of affability and ability made Stewart one of the Tour's most popular players, both on the course and in the clubhouse. Even when his game experienced roller-coaster years in the mid-'90s, Stewart never lost his zeal for life or his amiable approach to others. Yet it was during those ups and downs on the course that his life seemed enigmatic as well. It was as if he were searching for something.

Somewhere along his quest, Payne found what was missing. He renewed his relationship with God through Jesus Christ. The result was undeniable. Fans recognized it, as did the media and Payne's peers.

"We started to see something new; something totally different," said friend and fellow pro Paul Azinger. "We saw a man who was as interested in people as he was in golf. A man who played to win but truly loved others at the same time. Payne became gracious in victory and gracious in defeat. Only God could do that because only God changes hearts. Everyone who knew Payne saw this dramatic change in his life."

At the 1999 U.S. Open, Payne's newfound outlook took center stage. This was seemingly the moment he had been born for, and born again

for. In draining a fifteen-foot putt on the final hole, Stewart became a champion once again. In victory, he turned to the man he defeated, the father-to-be Phil Mickelson, grabbed both sides of his face, looked deep into his eyes, and said, "You're going to be a great father; you're going to be a great father!" and then hugged him. At once, everyone knew something was different about Payne.

They also noticed his WWJD bracelet ("What Would Jesus Do?"), which was a new addition to the knickers and tam that had long been Payne's trademark tournament apparel. Early in the '99 season, Stewart's ten-year-old son, Aaron, had given his dad the bracelet and challenged him to let others know about his commitment to Christ. It was like telling a Sphinx to keep silent. Payne let the world know.

"There used to be a void in my life," he told the press shortly after the dramatic win. "The peace I have now is so wonderful. I don't understand how I lived so long without it. I'm proud of the fact that my faith in God is so much stronger, and I'm so much more at peace with myself than I've ever been in my life."

It certainly showed.

Payne Stewart had style and panache. He was a trendsetter and a non-conformist. In his career, he won three majors, eleven tournament titles overall, and three Skins Games. He was named to five Ryder Cup teams and made millions of dollars. As satisfying as those accomplishments were, Payne's personal triumphs made him stand out—a fact directly attributable to his burgeoning faith.

He was loved and showed the golf world the reality of God's love. He was unique and genuine. There will never be another quite like him.

"I thank God for Payne. We shared laughter, tears, victories, and defeats. After eighteen years, he's still the most beautiful man I've ever seen. Not for the way he looked on the outside, but for what was on the inside. Payne inspired hope. He saw failures only as temporary setbacks. If he were here today, he would say, 'Don't ever give up. Don't ever lose hope. Your future is not measured by your past. With God's help, you can live and die victoriously.' I count it an honor that God would choose my husband to tell the world how much He really loves them."

TRACEY STEWART [WIFE]

"If you haven't made your peace with God, then you'd better make it....I go out there, and I'm not worried about what's going to happen. I'm going to be taken care of. I've made my peace with God."

PAYNE STEWART
[SHORTLY BEFORE HIS DEATH]

"If golf was an art, Payne Stewart was the color. Payne Stewart had style in the clothes he wore. Payne had a beautiful golf swing. He had a lot of heart. He touched many lives....I don't see how we could possibly forget Payne Stewart."

PAUL AZINGER

"It is important that we not lose sight of the most important things about Payne Stewart: that he was a man of great faith; that he was a devoted, compassionate, and most energetic husband and father; and that he was a man of tremendous generosity....Payne Stewart as a professional and a champion is irreplaceable."

TIM FINCHEM, PGA Commissioner

"Golf will miss Payne. I'll miss him as a friend. He had style. He had charisma. He wasn't afraid to say what was on his mind. Those were all endearing qualities to golf fans. They were endearing to his fellow players, too....I wish I could tell him once more how much he meant to me."

HAL SUTTON

"I know he lived his life trying to answer that question in his own life—what would Jesus do? That's what Payne Stewart tried to do. I think we can all learn from that."

TOM LEHMAN

STEVE RIACH is president and cofounder of VisionQuest Communications Group, Inc., a media company based in Dallas, Texas. Along with being a popular writer and speaker, Steve is a an award-winning producer, director and writer of films, videos and television and radio programming, making him one of the leading sports content creators in America. He and business partner John Humphrey have built one of the nation's preeminent positive-values sports media companies. Steve and his wife Wendy, and children Kristen, Joshua and Elissa reside in Colleyville, Texas.

TOM DIPACE is one of America's premier sports photographers. For the past 12 years, his work has been seen in such noted publications as *USA Today, Baseball Weekly, Sports Illustrated, SPORT Magazine, ESPN The Magazine.* and *Beckett Monthly.* Tom regularly covers all 30 teams in Major League Baseball and all 31 teams in the NFL. He also covers a variety of other sports including pro and college basketball, tennis, NASCAR, hockey, and golf. He has over one million stock images in his photo library. Tom and family reside in Lake Worth, Florida.

DID YOU KNOW

- The Romans during the reign of Caesar played a game resembling golf by striking a feather-stuffed ball with club-shaped branches.

- The Dutch played a similar game on their frozen canals about the fifteenth century, with cross-country variations popular in France and Belgium at the same time.

- In 1457, golf was banned in Scotland because it interfered with the practice of archery, which was vital to the defense effort. Nevertheless the Scots continued to brave the opposition of both Parliament and church by playing the game on seaside courses called links.

- Scotland boasts the world's oldest golf course, St. Andrews, used as early as the sixteenth century.

- Golf became firmly established in Great Britain by the seventeenth century when James VI of Scotland, later James I of England, was attracted to the sport.

- The Royal and Ancient Golf Club at St. Andrews, the cradle of golf, was founded in 1754.

- In the 1800s the gutta-percha ball ("gutty") replaced the feather-filled ball used for centuries.

- In 1860 the first British Open was played at Prestwick, Scotland.

- The first permanent golf club in North America, Canada's Royal Montreal Club, was founded in 1873.

- The first eighteen-hole course in the United States, the Chicago Golf Club, was founded near Wheaton, Illinois, in 1893.

- International golf competition dates from 1922, when teams of American and British amateurs first competed for the Walker Cup. Five years later the Ryder Cup series between professionals of the two nations was inaugurated.

- Walter Hagen was the first full-time tournament pro, beginning in 1919.

- In 1913 Francis Ouimet was the first amateur to win the U.S. Open.

- The National Golf Foundation estimates there are more than 20 million golfers in the U.S.

- Golf courses and practice facilities in the U.S. number about 15,000.

- Each year U.S. golfers spend nearly 600 million dollars for equipment.

- The standard cup in play is $4\frac{1}{4}$ inches in diameter and at least 4 inches deep.

- A maximum of fourteen clubs may be used in tournament play, most weighing 13 to $13\frac{1}{2}$ ounces.

- U.S. golf balls must be at least 1.68 inches in diameter and weigh not more than 1.62 ounces.